LAMBS TO
LEADERS

Mary,
Thanks for being wonderful,
your brightness adds to our
lives. I hope this book does the
same for you. Love Cliff

LAMBS TO LEADERS

Liberal Arts Majors in a Business Society

CLIFF OXFORD

Redwood Publishing, LLC
Orange County, California
info@redwooddigitalpublishing.com

Printed in the United States of America

Disclaimer: This book is designed to provide information and motivation to its readers. It is sold with the understanding that the author and publisher are not engaged to render any type of psychological, legal, or any other kind of professional advice. The content of each article is the sole expression and opinion of its author and is not meant to substitute for any advice from your healthcare professionals, lawyers, therapists, business advisors/partners, or personal connections.

ISBN 978-1-947341-57-9 (pb)
ISBN 978-1-947341-56-2 (ebook)

Book Designed by Redwood Publishing
(www.redwooddigitalpublishing.com)

First Edition

10 9 8 7 6   5 4 3 2 1

TABLE OF CONTENTS

CHAPTER 1

YOU ARE A BUSINESS NEWBIE. NOW WHAT?

I know you thought about being a doctor, a lawyer, or a movie star, or maybe you thought about owning a bar. Instead, you landed a spot in the business world. You got yourself a 9 to 5 corporate job or in some cases it might be a 9 to 9 if you landed in a tech startup or plan to start your own company.

This can be an upper not a downer if you read this book, understand the "biz playing field," and avoid making a few fatal mistakes.

This is a book about how to succeed in a setting where, right now, you may not understand what anybody is talking about half the time. Poly Sci 101 is Pluto compared to the job you are walking into on earth that first morning. In my experience as an employer in the business world, I've found that Liberal Arts majors can often be outstanding team members. We bring a diversity of life experience, curiosity and human interests that people who are thinking business from day one simply cannot match.

It's just that the people in the business world who love business have a huge advantage over you. They speak *the language of business*. They know what the terminology means. They can toss around acronyms like lottery numbers in an air machine.

This is not a book about how to get a job or how to get in a top tier business school. This book is meant to help you succeed after you get your foot in the door of either.

The truth of the matter is, I want you to quickly find your rhythm at work so you have the confidence to use your creativity to solve problems for your employer from the moment you first walk in the door or sign on from your computer to work from home. That is what will separate you from your newfound colleagues – by the way, think of them that way and not as friends. The high hurdle here is that not only are you new to business but the business environment is marked by rapidly changing threats and opportunities from competitors and demands from changing markets; most organizations can't handle decision-making in a totally rational way. Behind the curtain (the internal operations of a company) is an unstable environment where it is hard to get stuff done. Breaking news – most managers, starting from the top down, don't block out large chunks of time like you might think for planning, organizing, motivating and training as the books and pundits say they should. Their time is fragmented, often split between meeting after meeting, and usually frozen in "wait-and-see" decision-making. This means they don't spend time connecting with their team members and execution (i.e. getting work done to completion) often grinds to a halt. Here is the great news – while others wander in the face of this complexity, you can stand out as a success if you can intellectually and practically handle the five points below.

- Business Lingo – walk the walk and talk the talk
- Know how to negotiate for a win-win or no deal situation
- Survive the "Brilliant Jerk"
- Day 1 Ready
- Rules of the Road, Business Norms, Customs, and Etiquette

One more thing: if we get too deep in the weeds on any of the five topics – I will throw you a bone. Think of it as a quick relief from all the business stuff; I'll relate it to a more interesting subject in the liberal arts, like anthropology.

I'm not saying that by reading this book, you'll automatically become a top business expert, but I will give you the knowledge to level out the playing field and hold your own in the office. I'll also (hopefully) save you from asking those embarrassing questions like: "Does 'AP' mean Associated Press?" (The answer is: no, it means Accounts Payable.)

Who am I to write this book? I've been running, building, buying, selling, and coaching business owners for a long time. Long enough to recognize the unique value that Liberal Arts majors bring to an enterprise, and also long enough to see that unless you can toss the language around, you're not going to have much fun at work. By the way, I was also a Liberal Arts major before entering MBA school at Emory and working at UPS corporate at the same time. Honestly, I felt like I entered business school blind. Between the expected business norms and terminology, as a poly sci major, I sort of got lost my first year at school. But then I soon realized that not many in my class, or even at work, could do what we call the big three – speak, write, and be creative. What I am going to teach you in this book took me about a year to learn as I survived school and my first business job. Ultimately, I was able to thrive as the youngest district manager in UPS, where I was promoted seven times, and I went on to ace the second year of business school with distinction.

So enjoy a fast ramp to all of the peculiar definitions, philosophies, and pet peeve explanations that are used formally and casually in the business society every day. My goal is that with this newfound knowledge, you can jumpstart your new career or company.

CHAPTER 2

BASIC BUSINESS INSTINCTS

Here is the deal. First, you've got to understand the lingo of business – common terms in the business world – words and expressions. Some will be obvious; some less so. All are used with a frequency and flow that everyone with a business background knows what they mean. Master these terms and you're on your way to understanding what your boss, colleagues, and customers are talking about! Here's your first bone – an anthropology factoid. Although there are over 6,800 languages spoken each day, all can be traced back to a single common linguistic tribe called "proto." Humans have spoken as far back as 100,000 years ago in East Africa.

Aha Moment –

A moment of sudden realization, inspiration, insight, recognition, or understanding. You figure something out and the answer hits you belatedly. (This is also known as a "Come to Jesus" Moment.)

All Hands On Deck –

In business, usually put in the context of an upcoming meeting; signals all rank and file and titles should attend and pay attention. Tenacious D's song "All Hands On Deck" says it well, "All in front, all in back, just like that."

Assets –

What the company owns, including cash, real estate, and equipment.

Attachment –

"See attachment." This signals to the recipient that there is a file accompanying your email or embedded into the email itself. If you're sending an email with this note, take a breath to check and verify that the attachment is included. Don't shoot blanks where no attachment exists, causing everybody to scramble and find your email. A good rule of thumb is not to trust that technology is automatic in business. Verify and have back-up plans. Here is another bone – the French write "cf pj" which means to "see attachment." Even more than a bone, you now know how to impress the French guy or girl across the room!

Balance Sheet –

A ledger that shows the assets (what the company owns) and liabilities (what the company owes) of a given company. In short, it balances out a company's assets and liabilities to show the health and worth of the company.

Base Salary –

Your periodic total gross pay, which is deposited into your checking account. Your base salary does not include benefits, bonuses, or other potential compensation from your employer.

Best in Class –

Business is divided into categories like medical, manufacturing, hospitality, etc., and "Best in Class" is to proclaim that they have the best company in that category. A free market allows any business to say they are best in class and the customer decides who is.

Best of Breed –

Product considered to be the best of it's kind. (Not to be confused with "Best in Class.")

Bleeding Edge –

Any technology so new that it may not work right, causing people who buy it to have to spend more money to make use of those technologies. There is typically a high risk involved when going in on "bleeding edge" technology. By the way, everyone who creates a tech startup claims that his or her company is "bleeding edge." Some people can also refer to this as "best in breed."

Boilerplate –

An agreement or contract that has standard terms and conditions that can be reused on all agreements.

Boiler Room –

An infamous, jam-packed bottom floor packed with hyper-aggressive salespeople who are peddling deals on stocks, software, technologies, etc. If you plan on going into any sales role, there are two must-see movies – 1) Boiler Room with Ben Affleck and 2) Glengarry Glen Ross with Alec Baldwin. Both are great stories on what *not* to do in business, but both also have some grains of truth.

Boot-Strapping –

A startup that does not take outside capital and instead grows on its own money. Occasionally, a company will require a new product division to "boot-strap" it with little or no internal funding from the big company, often referred to as a "parent company."

Burn Rate –

How quickly a company is going through its cash – total expenses exceed total revenue.

C-Level Executives –

Also known as the "C-Suite." C means Chief, which is high and often highest on the totem pole in corporations.

CAO –

Chief Analytics Officer. A 3rd tier player at best. The title is typically given for recruitment and retention purposes only. Most don't even know what a CAO does.

CEO –

Chief Executive Officer. The ultimate boss. Remember that CEOs are human beings and would like it if you said hello if you run them in the hallway. Remember that as a sixth-round draft pick, quarterback Tom Brady told Patriots owner Robert Kraft, "I will show you why this is the best decision the team has ever made." CEOs like confidence. Don't try to be their best friend – not going to happen. But definitely let them know you're in the building.

CFO –

Chief Financial Officer. Usually runs accounting and finance function. Heavyweight. They control the money.

Chief Sales Officer or Chief Revenue Officer –

In larger companies, these roles are not as important as you might think and those who hold them are basically order-fillers. If you've got what everybody wants, you don't have to do a heck of a lot of selling. On the other hand, in an entrepreneurial company, this is a very important position as nothing happens inside the company until you sell something.

CIO –

Chief Information Officer. Twenty years ago, these were big dudes, but they have taken a backseat in today's world as IT (Information Technology) has become more of a utility for the business. In the past, CIOs made tons of bad calls on software, and they are typically among the shortest tenured people in the C-Suite. Don't hitch your wagon to a CIO.

CMO –

Chief Marketing Officer. Was once a second-tier player in companies, but now has stepped up to top tier with the saturation of digital commerce. Heavyweight – spends a lot of money.

COO –

Chief Operating Officer. Often considered 2nd in charge. I call them "A Number Two Who Can Do."

Cloud –

This has nothing to do with the weather. The Cloud is a shared pool of computer system resources that companies can use over the Internet without having to build out their own computer infrastructure. Think about your electricity bill. You don't have to have your own power plant. You just buy power from some outside entity, and as a result, your lights are on and you can recharge your phone. Cloud computing is basically the same concept for companies. "Cloud" just sounds a lot cooler than "Basic Utility." As far as computers in a company, almost everything is "in the cloud" – don't ask IT where the cloud is…they don't know.

Come to Jesus Meeting –

In the business world, this term indicates a meeting to solve big differences on delicate ongoing issues.

Comp Plan –

Short for compensation plan, which explains how an employee will be paid. This includes bonuses, commissions, base salary, stock, benefits, and days off (holidays and vacation).

Confidentiality Agreements –

Contracts used to protect trade secrets and expertise from being misappropriated or misused by those who have access to them.

Consultants –

Companies don't hire them, but instead contract with them for a specific period of time to deliver general and specific expertise. They usually have higher access to management than project level and middle managers employed inside of the company. By the way, don't freak out and assume they are there to take your job – most make too much money doing what they're doing to quit. If you want to watch a good movie about consultants, check out Up in the Air with George Clooney.

Consultative Sales –

A type of selling that implies a longer sales cycle or period of time from meeting the prospect to closing the deal. A transactional salesperson gets the sales contract signed, or gets a no and it's on to the next deal. A consultative salesperson wants to show you how the product or service will benefit you, and will be there to support it after the sale. It's rare for one salesperson to have both consultative and transactional skills.

Conventional Culture –

Forget about traditional, people who do what is expected and common. Conventional culture isn't necessarily a bad or negative thing. It's like wearing a long white dress to your wedding – this is a conventional and expected norm.

Copyrights –

Copyrights protect the expression of ideas. You can copyright a novel or a song you wrote so that no one else can profit from it for a given period of time.

Corporate B.S. –

It is basically where people talk in corporate clichés. Here is a great example of jargon:

Thought leaders seeking organic growth should be laser-focused on customer-centric solutions. So lean in and move the needle. Solutioning is a value add that demonstrates core competency, strategic fit and your ability to think outside the box. Corporate values demand that you give 110%. Great communication is an area of opportunity that's not above your pay-grade.

So be a growth hacker. Take some Q&A.

Corporate Values –

Theoretically, the operating principles, philosophies, or prophesies that guide a company.

Cottage Business –

Often used in a way to throw shade. A condescending classification of a given company that means it is a nice little business that will never be massive. Also known as a "mom-and-pop" or a "Lifestyle Business." Owners of successful cottage businesses often work fewer hours and can make a ton of money. Their problem is that a small change or ripple in the market could blow them away.

Critical Success Factors –

Attributes or elements that will make or break a new project or change a business.

Culture –

How the work gets done in a company under a certain style of leadership.

Customer Churn Rate –

Churn rate means how many customers you lose after they have tried the product or service for a given period of time. Churn rates are associated with companies that have "subscription income," meaning people who pay monthly or annually on an ongoing basis for what you offer. Cell phone companies, Dollar Shave Club, and clothing companies like Stitch Fix. High churn = not good.

Cutting Edge –

When something is at the latest or most advanced stage in development. This is different from "bleeding edge" as that specifically refers to technology. Cutting edge can be anything from processes to technology to art.

Dotted Line –

In an organizational chart, a solid line indicates the relationship between managers and their reports (the people who report to that manager). A dotted line report indicates an employee who has an implied level of accountability to another person but is not a direct report for that manager.

Drip-feed –

Process of slowly releasing and scheduling information for the future. Very likely related to a discussion about scheduling social media posts or a prolonged payment process to a supplier.

Due Upon Receipt –

Meaning payment is due when the receiver receives the invoice, which means they should stroke a check immediately. They rarely do. From the smallest mom-and-pop to the Fortune 500, business is a game of cash flow float – get as much cash in as fast as possible and send out cash as late as possible.

Entrepreneur –

Someone who starts companies if you listen to media and Fortune 500 C-Suite. By the way, anybody can do that. A *real* entrepreneur is someone who can get the maximum change or output from minimum resources. This often involves creating a new business category or completely flipping a current business model on its head. It takes about six years of training for an entrepreneur to bloom a business.

ERP: Enterprise Resource Planning –

Software that integrates core business processes like production, accounting, and HR.

Financial Scale –

The time period when a company's production creates greater profits at a rate faster than the cost of their expenses to produce. Airlines scale horribly – they can only get so many seats on a plane and tech companies like Facebook scale well – a lot more users added at a little cost. If you land in tech keep this quote in your back pocket: "Our product scales like the ocean."

Freemium –

You give the basic product away for free and then try to up-sell paid features to your customers. The "do or die" part of this business model is your "conversion rate," which indicates how many freebie people you convert to paying customers.

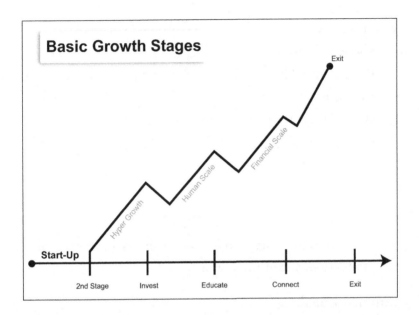

Growth Hacking –

A buzzword meaning that someone claims to be really good at creating growth for a company, through marketing or other means. Word mostly used by 2nd and 3rd tier consultants. Stay away from it and people who use it.

Growth –

Cubic growth: In business, it's called "Hockey Stick Growth" and it is one of the most commonly used terms to describe a pattern of growth. The idea is that things like users, page view, or revenue stays at the same level, then once an inflection point is hit, growth takes off at an exponential rate. When growth is slow, the great excuse is "waiting on the hockey stick."

Exponential Growth: In business, it means explosive growth. Technically, a multiple rate of change in growth per instant or unit of time. I would stick with "fast growth," in case some Brilliant Jerk (discussed in Chapter 8) might ask you to explain the mathematics of it. That won't happen, and 95% of people in business could not give you that definition. So if people say they're looking for exponential growth, it means they just want to grow fast. Most of you had to at least take pre-algebra so you would remember the term square line $9^2=81$ – same concept as exponential.

Hyper Growth: This occurs when a company figures out how to deliver a unique solution to an underserved market. Think Uber when it first opened.

Linear growth: Another way in business of saying slow growth. The business world and Wall Street frown on linear growth, even though it's still…growth. Linear growth specifically means growing by the same amount in each unit of time. Which means as you get larger, your % rate slows. Don't freak out – only one more geometry term. See the chart next page.

Has Legs –

This means that a concept or plan is credible and can stand on its own merit. The phrase is declining in popularity – probably due to the #MeToo movement.

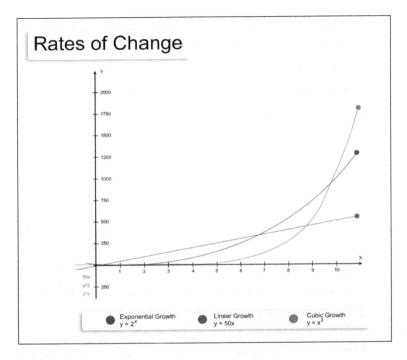

H Bomb –

Dropping an "H Bomb" is when a colleague "drips out" the details of their college and eventually, they drop the bomb that they graduated from Harvard. It usually goes something like this – first they mention they went to school Up North, and then upon further questioning, they say they attended school in Boston, then it turns to Cambridge, before they finally say Harvard.

Headspace –

This used to mean that "stuff" that occupies your mind but now, it refers to an app on your phone for meditation.

Considered a gateway drug to silent retreats (over 40 million downloads).

HR –

Human Resources. Where hiring, firing, or complaints within the company are handled. They've tried to give these folks C-Suite titles like Chief People Officer, but it hasn't stuck. The heads of HR are top tier players because they know all the company gossip and are always in the room when layoffs or major hiring initiatives take place. HR used to be called Personnel, and their main job was to recruit talent for the company. They outsourced that function to staffing companies and now do the more fun stuff. It's the lala land of business if they have no direct recruiting responsibility.

Human Scale –

It is a beautiful point in business – you can add people and add profits to the company bottom line rather than losses. Prior to human scale, a business can grow but also be in danger of going under due to the investments needed in people & infrastructure to keep up with growth.

We wade through these terms. If you landed a job in a company with less than 50 million in total revenues, you will hear the word "scale" more times than Jimmy Carter said "Social Security" in his 1980 debate with then-Governor Ronald Reagan, who would reply, "There he goes again." That was another bone; millennials – Google it!

Infrastructure —

Your house has infrastructure – plumbing, wiring, driveway, sprinkler system, an elevator if you live in an apartment building. Those are the "guts" of the house, and they allow it to function as a house so that you can live in it. A company's infrastructure is the basic physical and organizational structure and technologies needed so that the company can run. If a company grows too quickly or rolls out too many projects too quickly, the infrastructure can become overwhelmed and the company blows up faster than a garage band's amplifier in their dad's basement. Keep in mind that just as companies can fail because they have too few customers, they can also collapse because they have too many and the infrastructure cannot keep up.

Invoice —

A bill delivered to the receiver of goods or services.

Jack Dorsey —

Founder of Twitter. He is cool and obscure and you'll get some brownie points for mentioning his name organically in conversation.

Legacy —

Software, hardware, or media that has been technologically superseded but difficult to replace because of wide use. Mainframe computing and broadcast channels are two great examples of legacy systems and legacy media. The word has spilled over to how entrepreneurs and executives see their profile post mortem.

Letter of Agreements —

Binding contracts that appear in the form of correspondence or letters as opposed to something that looks like a formal contract.

Liabilities —

What the company owes.

Liar's Poker —

Bluffing with a big lie to win and game over.

Like a Boss —

Means someone handles a job impressively. Use at your own risk. A trendy and shallow term, to say the least.

Loss Leader Pricing —

Selling something at a loss as a marketing expense to bring in customers to whom you can sell more stuff at higher margins. Gas stations sell gas cheap so you stop and go in and buy the high margin potato chips.

Low Ball Offer —

An offer significantly below a seller's asking price.

Low Hanging Fruit —

Easy wins or the simplest things your company can do to bring cash in the door or reap the rewards of a new project or opportunity. Sometimes low hanging fruit is very hard to identify and even harder to harvest. Mark my words, the guy who does the least will say, "We can't get to the low hanging fruit because we are tripping over watermelons," which means we cant see huge opportunities right under our feet.

M&A –

Mergers and Acquisitions. Basically the buying and selling of companies. Think of real estate agents buying and selling homes, but don't mention the analogy to a finance person, because they hate it. Investment bankers are the realtors in that model – they are the ones who represent buyers and sellers when companies are bought and sold.

M&As are popular in business because instead of finding say, $50 million worth of new income, you can buy a company that brings in $50 million a year and just like that, your company grew overnight by $50 million.

Of course, your company may blow the acquisition altogether and lose a ton of money, which happens most of the time, so M&A makes a lot of money for the people who actually do the deals, but not always a lot of money for the companies that get bought or get sold.

Market Cap –

For publicly traded companies, the market cap means what the company is worth. You multiply the number of shares outstanding or owned by people or institutions, times the share price. That's the market cap. 1 million shares outstanding x share price of $100.00 = 1 Billion.

Matrix –

Not the movie, but a different kind of organizational structure in which the reporting relationships (bosses and workers) are set up as a grid instead of a traditional hierarchy where each employee reports to a boss. In a matrix, employees can have dual bosses, like a functional manager and a product manager, or even multiple competing bosses. So employees have to work autonomously but be in contact with many people.

Monetize –

How you plan to make money on your idea. If you have a great idea, the finance people will say, "How are you going to monetize it?"

Moon Shot –

Lofty target or goals – the term comes from Apollo 11 mission where man went to the moon.

Moving Parts –

A messy business that is all entangled and sloppy. When there are a lot of moving parts and things are complicated, somebody is going to lose a lot of money. Similar to "hair on the deal," which means a lot of complications that no one wants to bother with.

Ninja –

A term of affection to describe someone who is very good at a task.

No Man's Land –

A market space of uncertainty, a period of inaction after planning a strategy, or a company that's too big to be small and too small to be big and occurs after hyper-growth and prior to human scale.

Non-Compete Agreements –

Prevents founders, managers, and employees from going into competition by starting or joining another company in the same market space.

Off The Grid –

When somebody on your team says they are going "off the grid," it means they plan to be off email and unavailable via their cell phone for a certain period of time. Don't go off the grid your first year – don't bring it up.

Oku –

Give a little more now to get a lot more later.

Org Chart –

A diagram that shows the structure of an organization and who reports to whom. The CEO is at the top of every Org chart. Everyone in the C-Suite normally reports to the CEO or COO.

Organic Growth –

Not something you buy at Whole Foods. It's where a company finds a new customer "organically" – and adds their fees to total revenue. Organic growth means a customer was obtained naturally and without the use of paid marketing or paid content. The opposite of organic growth is buying growth through an acquisition. You'll typically hear this phrase thrown around in the marketing department.

Paper it –

Translate a verbal agreement into a document.

Parent Company –

A company that owns another company which is deemed a subsidiary of the parent company.

Patent –

A government authority or license conferring a right or title for a set period, especially the sole right to exclude others from making, using, or selling an invention.

Ramen Profitable –

A company just profitable enough to cover costs and basic living expenses for everyone working there. They may not be burning cash, but they sure aren't killing it yet.

Reinvent the Wheel –

Waste a great deal of money or effort when creating something that already exists. When said in business, it mostly refers to not adding new expenses.

Repurpose and Repackage –

Taking an old idea, dress it up, and repackage it in a new way.

Sandbagging –

A pretend weakness to have an easy goal to make.

Scale –

A fancy way to say that you can grow and increase profit at the same time.

Shares –

One of the equal parts to which a company is divided, entitling the owner to a portion of possible profits and dividends or a portion of equity if the company is sold.

Side Bar –

An informal meeting between two people right before or after a planned meeting.

Silicon Valley North –

Coders and capitalists from Microsoft and Amazon.

Social Capital –

Bragging value among peers where the value is highly perceived by society such as having a prestigious law firm represent you or having children attend Ivy League school.

Strategy –

The plan of action to achieve a goal, which is typically different than that of the competition. As opposed to tactics (see below).

Square the Circle –

Do the impossible.

SWOT Analysis –

This means you are assessing a company's strengths, weaknesses, opportunities, and threats. There is really no wrong answer as long as what you say makes sense and isn't totally clear to the people you're reporting to. To do a SWOT Analysis, you draw a cross as below and divide it into four equal sections for each word.

Here is my SWOT Analysis of a large Cola company:

Strength – Market Share, Size, Top 5 company brand in world, global logistics

Weaknesses – Bureaucratic and slow

Opportunities – Wide distribution, bring new product to market fast, acquire emerging brands, R&D budgets

Threats – Inside management team, niche products entering markets, health and wellness crusades

If you think you see the right opportunity, then ask your boss whether you should do a SWOT Analysis. If she says yes, you look like a genius. If she gives you a hard time and says something patronizing like, "Listen to the Liberal Arts major!" just smile and own it. Just say, "I'm reading ahead to keep up with you guys."

Tactics —

The steps you take to achieve the goal. "Thinking strategically" means looking at the big picture. "Thinking tactically" means looking at the various steps you will take — the tactics — in order to achieve the overall strategy.

Terms & Conditions —

Explains the ifs, ands, and buts of the agreement or provides terms on an invoice that details how the receipt is to be paid.

Trademarks —

A symbol, word, or words, legally registered or established by use as representing a company or product.

Valuation —

What investors think a private company is worth. Just as a home has a value, so do companies. If a company has had an IPO or Initial Public Offering and is now a publicly traded company, the company valuation is tabulated on stock exchange. Private company valuations are up to interpretation. Here is what IRS says: "The **fair market value** of a private company is the price between a **motivated buyer** and a **willing seller**, neither being under any compulsion to buy or to sell and both having reasonable knowledge of relevant facts."

In short, a private company is worth what someone is willing to write you a check for it.

It is not a set mathematical number like a public company where the price of a company is worth stock price x number of outstanding shares.

Vendor —

A person or company offering something for sale.

You've Got This —

A patronizing way of telling a colleague that he or she is up to a given task. Only use this playfully, if at all. If someone says it to you, they are probably backstabbing you in the break room without your knowledge.

15 Days (30 Days or 45 Days) —

Instead of being "due upon receipt," payment is due in 15 days, or 30 days, or 45 days, or whenever noted. If a bill is not due or owed upon receipt, then the receiver puts it into their "Accounts Payable" system as basically an IOU. While the sender of the bill considers it an "Account Receivable" or a "receivable," it means somebody owes the company this money.

CHAPTER 3

LET THE LOVE FLOW– BIZ ABBREVIATIONS

In business, money follows cool and C-Suite leaders yearn for both. Abbreviations are like sunglasses on the beach. Everywhere in sight and you don't want to be standing there like a deer in headlights trying to look this stuff up on your phone. Not cool. Master these abbreviations and you can walk the talk at the office.

B-to-B –

Business to Business. Your company sells things to other companies. For example, Paychex does payroll services for other companies. This is a pure "B-to-B play." Consumers don't need payroll services. Note the spelling – B-to-B (or sometimes, it's written as B2B). Make sure you get it right.

B-to-C –

Business to Consumer (or B2C). Your company sells stuff to the masses or niches of consumers. So figure out whether you are B-to-B or B-to-C before you walk in the door.

B-to-E –

Business to everybody and merges B2B and B2C to create one selling platform.

BD –

Business Development. A fancy title for a salesperson.

BFD –

Big Frickin' Deal (polite form).

CPA –

Certified Public Accountant. They are respected inside companies because you have to be smart to pass the CPA exam for a license to practice accounting. It is similar to the bar exam for lawyers, but harder.

CRM –

Customer Resource Management technology. This is a software program that enables you to keep track of people & projects with which you are in business. CRM allows sales, marketing, and customer service teams to connect with other internal departments within a company and deliver sales, service, and follow-up to customers. It's a contact system that keeps track of notes, actions, and appointments between your company and your customers.

If you called Amazon and said you never received your package, they would log your complaint in their CRM system to keep track of it. If you called a company and said that you were interested in buying their product, they would log you as a prospect in their CRM system.

SalesForce has become the largest of all CRM companies and is synonymous with CRM, just as FedEx is synonymous for sending overnight letters.

Anyone who uses a CRM system is called a "user." Ask your boss if you will be a CRM user. If yes, ask if you can take the tutorial before you start work.

Your job on day one is to know what CRM stands for, what it does, which one your company uses, whether you are supposed to use it, and if so, how.

CX –

Customer Experience. This is a big up and coming buzzword. Customer experience means everything that happens from the first time that the customer visits the website or calls the 800 number through buying, calling the help desk, or whatever.

FMA –

First Mover Advantage. The first company to enter a new market segment is said to have "first mover advantage."

You can often overcome first mover advantage by spending resources to educate the market as to why they should buy from you. This happens all the time. FMA can apply to a start-up or Fortune 500 rolling out a new product.

GC –

General Counsel. A lawyer who is hired as an employee of the company to administer contracts, employee agreements, and other documents. The C-Suite typically sees them as chief clerk and not a major player. Despite that, they could be a good person to know.

IPDE –

A problem-solving methodology: Identify, Predict, Decide & Execute. Identify the problem, predict outcomes, decide on an answer, and execute the details.

IPO –

Initial Public Offering. This is where a private company "goes public" and sells its shares to the public for the first time. From that moment on, the company is known as a public company.

Companies can be "taken private," which means the management essentially buys it back from the public who own all the shares. Companies can also be "delisted" or thrown off a stock market if they fail to provide proper information to regulators.

KISS Method –

Keep It Simple, Stupid. Take complex problems, develop simple solutions and you are a genius in business. Merely pointing out complex problems, you are not doing anyone a favor.

LET –

"Leaving early today." Text and email only. Don't do this too often, by the way.

LOI –

Letter of Intent. Non-binding written agreement highlighting terms of a potential deal. A letter of intent is not a contract, and you don't get a commission on one.

OOO –

Out of Office. Never say this about yourself, because soon you will be OOJ (out of a job).

OT –

Overtime, meaning you get paid at a higher hourly rate after working more than 40 hours in one week. If you are salaried staff, by the way, you most likely don't get overtime. Sorry.

OTT: Over the Top –

Distribution of video on demand (VOD) and film content delivered via the Internet, instead of traditional cable or satellite paid TV service. Ex: Netflix, Hulu, Youtube.

PA –

Performance appraisal. An annual review of your work, which is actually a dying breed, because studies indicate that it is useless if done only once a year. Everybody prefers routine communication and feedback. Don't be surprised if your company doesn't do PAs or if you don't get much feedback unless you ask. That's just how it works.

PM –

Project Manager. They are typically mid-level managers and are responsible for getting things from point A to point B. PMs work with everybody in the company, from the marketing department to high-level executives. They are a highly valued skill set.

POC –

Point of Contact. The person or department serving as the coordinator or focal point of information concerning an activity or program. Job security occurs when you are the point of contact for a major account or client, and those people like you personally.

POS –

Point of Sale, where cash, credit, or trade is exchanged.

PR –

Public Relations. One of the most important functions a company performs. The CEO should be chief of PR, as Bill Gates and Steve Jobs were, and as Jeff Bezos of Amazon is. If you land in PR and you're not in love with it, try to move elsewhere. PR is always the first to be hit by layoffs.

R&D –

Research and Development. Highly likely that you are not going here. Just practice rolling off R&D off your tongue 3 or 4 times because the abbreviation is a standard in American business.

RPA –

Robotics Process Automation. Artificial intelligence.

SEO –

Search Engine Optimization. This means figuring out how to appear at the top of the page when someone Googles your company name, product, service, category, or even asks a question that is remotely relevant to what you do. Because there are constant scams involving people charging huge amounts of money for SEO and delivering nothing, the term is a little bit disreputable. But at the same time, if you have SEO, you're very fortunate. There is no magic formula other than to pay for it or put out great content that attracts herds of people. You are not going to outsmart Google.

SM –

Social Media. You will only see this abbreviated in a text, written report, or email. In conversation, people always say, "social media."

SMB –

Small to medium business. These businesses are bigger than you think. A $50 million business is considered a medium-sized business, and a $10 million business is considered small. Oracle has large, Fortune 500 clients, but also has an SMB division to sell a simpler version of its product to those smaller companies.

UV –

Unique Visitor. A term used in web marketing indicating an individual who visits a site at least once within a defined reporting period, usually monthly. If that same email address visits the site a hundred times during the reporting period, that person is still counted only once as a visitor.

VC –

Venture Capitalist. Individuals or groups that finance start-ups. They are often called Vulture Capitalists because they take so much of the company's equity. On *Shark Tank*, the Sharks are essentially venture capitalists.

Text and Email Abbreviations

BID – Break it down

COB – Close of business

EOD – End of day

EOW – End of week

FWIW – For what it's worth

IAM – In a meeting

IMO – In my opinion

NRN – No reply necessary

NSFW – Not safe for work

CHAPTER 4

ACCOUNTING IS THE BEASTIE BOYS OF BUSINESS

Most Liberal Arts majors avoid accounting like the flu. But accounting is to business what Latin is to the English language – the root of everything else. It is also as close as anything to a business science in its objectives to accurately measure money.

You need to know the term GAAP, which stands for Generally Accepted Accounting Practices, and it's pronounced just like the store, Gap. Accountants say that something is "good GAAP" when they see a practice in the measurement of money – income, expenses, sales, whatever – that match with generally accepted accounting practices. For the most part, accountants keep it straight and don't let fluffy words like "deep dive" fly, unless they are hanging out with the marketing folks, trying to impress the big boss, or have a romantic interest with someone in another department.

The good news is that you don't need to know how to do accounting or balance a ledger, but you do need to know certain accounting terms. Here they are:

AP –

Accounts Payable. (Worth repeating.) It is where suppliers and customers send their bill to the company to get paid. Most companies will wait at least thirty days to pay, so the bill resides in accounts payable until the company cuts the check or wires it. Think of it as your desk drawer at home where the electricity bill might sit for a while until you write a check for it or pay it online. By the way, don't confuse it with Associated Press.

AR –

Accounts Receivable. (Worth repeating.) When the supplier or customer bills the company – they don't want it floating in thin air and hope to get paid for it. They make a record of it called AR, which is basically an IOU because no cash has been collected. As soon as cash comes in the door, AR disappears. AP and AR are important terms and you need to recognize them. Sometimes Liberal Arts majors confuse AR with AI, or Artificial Intelligence. Don't do that.

Audit –

Methodical reviews by an independent third party of a company's accounts or financial situations.

Balance Sheet –

A balance sheet gives a snapshot of a business' financial status at a given time. Balance sheets include assets and liabilities.

If you ran a root beer stand, for example, your balance sheet would show assets like the wooden stand you built and your cash register. It would also show liabilities like your monthly payments (rent, electricity, etc.). If someone were looking to buy your root beer stand business, they'd want to look at your balance sheet to determine how financially healthy your business is and if your assets outweigh your liabilities.

Benchmarking –

Benchmarking is the process of comparing your company's performance metrics to others in your industry. Benchmarking helps you assess how your business is doing and competing. Benchmarking also serves as the foundation for most bonus programs.

Bottom line/net profit –

The "bottom line" refers to the last line of a business' balance sheet: the net profit. This number shows the total amount of money a business has earned in a month once expenses and COGS have been taken out.

"Bottom line" in business, outside of financial definition, also means final decision or final point of clarity to be made.

Cash Flow –

Cash flow is the movement or flow of money in and out of a business during a specific period of time (usually a month). A business' cash flow is measured by comparing its available cash at the beginning and end of the month. "Cash flow positive" means the amount of cash coming into the business was greater than the amount of money going out of the business.

Collateral –

An asset pledged for a loan or liability. Sometimes you hear a CEO say, "At one point, it got so bad that I had to use my house as collateral for a loan."

COGS (Cost of Good Sold) –

The acronym C.O.G.S. rhymes with "bogs" when pronounced. A marketing manager might throw this term around to impress the CFO or a controller might ask you, "What is the COGS?" It is the total cost to produce or provide and includes labor, materials, and any costs to bring to market.

Compound Interest –

Calculated on the principal amount and also the accumulated interest of the previous period.

CPA –

Certified Public Accountant. Professionals who by training and certification are qualified to audit a company's financial statements.

Cram Down –

Refers to a negotiation where one party has so much leverage over the other that it can dictate terms and extract every possible concession from the other side. Venture capitalists use this as a legitimate practice, but don't you use it. No one will like you.

Deck –

A Powerpoint presentation made to investors or buyers. Don't say Powerpoint. Say Deck. You will sound smarter.

Definitive Agreement –

A document defining the final terms of an agreement between buyer and seller. Mutually binding.

Exit Strategy –

How you will get out of a market or a business and get liquid (which means cash out), instead of leaving with nothing, which is called a Flame Out.

FIFO –

First In First Out. An accounting measurement of how a company receives and dispenses inventory. For example, the first product received at the store is the first product sold off the shelf.

Gross Margin –

The difference between revenue and COGS divided by revenue. It is a percent value of profit. Gross margin is determined by subtracting the cost of goods sold (COGS) from your revenue and dividing that number by your total revenue. The resulting percentage shows how valuable a sale is.

For your root beer stand, your gross margin is 73%, meaning that 73% of every dollar you make is gross profit (note: not net profit).

Gross Profit –

Refers to the money a company earns, represented as a whole dollar amount. Shows a monetary amount. Gross profit is the amount of money a business earns in a given period minus the cost of goods sold (COGS).

When you subtract COGS ($26.25) from your revenue ($100), you get your Gross Profit: $73.75

Hockey Stick Growth –

(Worth repeating.) Imagine a hockey stick superimposed on a graph. You've got the blade at the bottom, and then the hockey stick itself going up from the right of the blade. "Hockey stick growth" means that the company doesn't grow, doesn't grow, doesn't grow, and then suddenly explodes. Everybody loves hockey stick growth. It is very close to cubic growth in geometry.

Inc. –

An abbreviation for incorporation, which means the process of starting a company as a legal corporation.

Income Statement –

An income statement (also known as a Profit and Loss statement or "P&L") shows a business' revenue and expenses over a period of time.

The income statement for your rootbeer stand would show what you spent, what you earned, and whether you made or lost money that month.

In the Black –

When a company is making money.

In the Red –

When a company is losing money.

IP –

Intellectual property, which can be protected by a patent. A secret formula like the recipe for KFC chicken, or Coca-Cola, is a company's intellectual property. In the technology realm, IP means Internet Protocol, which is an address with a bunch of numbers and periods that indicates your laptop or desktop.

JV –

Joint Venture. A project where two companies or teams contribute different skill sets but share in revenue, costs, and overall results.

Lean Start-up –

The core mission to prove the business concept as quickly and cheaply as possible.

Leverage –

A big boy finance word meaning to use something – technology, volume, and so on – to your advantage so you can grow revenue and profits at a faster rate than your expenses.

LIFO –

Last in First Out. The opposite of FIFO – the last product put in inventory is the first out the door.

Liquidity –

How easily you can convert an asset or stock certificate into cash. For example, stocks on the New York Stock Exchange are extremely liquid, because you can buy and sell shares of those companies at will. A privately held company also has stock ownership, but that stock ownership typically does not change hands until someone buys the company. So that is considered an illiquid investment. This is why business owners love IPOs or Initial Public Offerings – it creates liquidity for the owners and shareholders.

LOI –

(Worth repeating.) Letter of Intent. This is a nonbinding documented agreement that covers the terms and conditions, which two parties intend to formalize in a legally binding agreement at a later date. A definitive agreement is a binding agreement – the final terms agreed upon by the two parties.

Negative Cash Flow –

You've got more money going out the door than coming in, which can lead to disaster and bankruptcy. This leads to the term "cash is king," which means getting cash is supreme to all other strategies.

Positive Cash Flow –

You've got more money coming in the door than going out. Nice!

Recurring Revenue –

Recurring revenue is money the company can count on in every time period. If you join a gym and sign a twelve-month contract, and you'll be making payments monthly, the company considers your twelve months of payments as recurring revenue. This way, they can figure out how many trainers they can hire, how much new equipment they can buy, and so on.

Recurring revenue is often tied to subscription business models, which is why if you stop subscribing to a magazine or newspaper, they will hunt you down like a savage beast. Companies that don't have recurring revenue have to go out and hunt new revenue just to stay in business. Recurring revenue rocks in business.

Revenue/Sales —

The words are interchangeable. This is the pure dollar amount a business takes in a given period of time – the amount of money earned before subtracting any expenses.

Ex. If you sell 100 glasses of root beer in a month at $1 per glass, your monthly revenue is $100.00. Your monthly sales are $100.00 A good saying in start-up companies is that revenue can solve a lot of problems and lack of it can cause a lot of problems.

ROI —

Return on Investment. How much you put in and what you take out. If you put $100 into a checking account and earn $3 in interest, your ROI on the $100 was $3. You can invest that same $100 in the stock market for a potentially higher ROI, but you will be running a bigger risk.

Runway —

How much time a company has until the cash or time runs out. This can apply both to a start-up as well as to a new project at a big company.

Seed Capital —

Money invested in a project or company before they have a fully developed product. It gets its name from seed corn— good quality corn set aside for seed.

Simple Interest —

Calculated on the principal or original amount of loan.

Term Sheet —

A bullet point document outlining the terms and conditions of a business agreement. It's like a guidebook in preparation of a proposed final agreement.

Vulture Capitalists —

A demeaning term to describe venture capitalists because of how much money and large percentage of the company they require to invest.

CHAPTER 5

MARKETING GENIUS IS THE RAREST BIRD IN BUSINESS

Best sales line in business, "You have a great vision—
you just need a little help getting there."

In the hunt for company talent, a true marketer is the rarest bird of them all. And on top of that, when companies get very close on price and product, it all comes down to marketing for who wins. Just because you have the best product out there doesn't mean that you will make the most money. Often the best product or service, for the business naïve, is equivalent to the birds and the bees story in nature. Marketing wins even if the product or service being marketed is of lesser quality or a more expensive price. The good news is that a Liberal Arts major has a better chance of being a marketing leader than an MBA grad. Here's an excerpt from an article I wrote for Forbes that explains why:

"When I am looking and interviewing for a marketing genius, I immediately disqualify anybody with a marketing degree because the business schools have incorrectly trained their students (and it takes too long to un-train them.) I am not picking on academia here because the schools get an "A" in training accountants. Here are a few guidelines to find this rare bird, the marketing genius, that can help you grow your company as big as the exponential ideas behind it (we'll just assume that you have the infrastructure and leadership team it will take to get there):

1. They are typically introverts who can fake being an extrovert.

2. They are prone to talking and thinking out loud even when alone.

3. They are customer advocates. They understand and apply hidden harmony marketing (customers surmise and realize you are great instead of you telling them you are).

4. They have a strong understanding of the world of ideas and a keen interest in what's hot, what's gossip, what's happening and what's relevant to audiences.

5. A true marketing genius is a voracious reader and pop culture fanatic.

6. They know how to sell intangibles, which is why sales teams love the marketing genius.

7. They are tenacious, persistent, persuasive, and not by any measure a pushover.

8. They are good storytellers. They get your attention and hold it in an authentic manner.

9. They want to make the world a smarter place and have a huge commitment to innovation.

10. They usually have some emotional baggage from childhood (did not grow up idealistically, so they had to make up their own world to live in).

Here is the business language of Marketing. Unless you are actually in the marketing department, wait at least 90 days before you start tossing these terms around. You need to know them now, but the smarter you try to sound, the dumber you will appear. Trust me.

Marketing —

This means promoting products and a company as a whole.

4 P's of Marketing —

The marketing mix is a foundational model for business schools to try to teach the discipline: Price, Product, Place, and Promotion. Mostly outdated, but still thrown around in marketing circles by marketing majors who answered the P's repeatedly on marketing quizzes.

Advanced Marketing —

I would argue Starbucks is a hospitality brand more than food. Your brand is emotionally linked to the company's shared values, which at Starbucks is a meeting place – stay a while even if you're not buying anything. I realize you cannot stay overnight, but Starbucks is more about an invite to visit rather than turning tables like fast food and other coffee shops. At any rate, Starbucks is in the inevitable position of being expensive and common to the masses, often called affordable luxury.

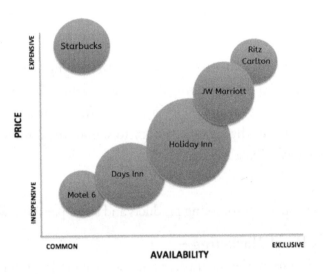

Advertorials –

Companies paying to publish content that looks like a real story written by a real journalist, but isn't.

Brainchild –

A product of one's creative work or thought and in business often a moniker given to someone in C-suite whose big idea flopped as a project.

Brand Positioning –

Sorry, I am going to be a little long-winded here because executives like to pontificate on this topic.

Here's the deal. ... Does your company compete on price, quality, or service? Typically, companies pick two out of the three. McDonald's competes on price and service. Ritz-Carlton competes on quality and service. If you are trying to compete on all three, you are doomed. It is why McDonald's doesn't sell steak (McRib doesn't count – parts unknown). A real gem in business is when a company is commonly exclusive like Apple and Starbucks – high price point but adopted by the masses. A company you want to work for is one who figures out who their customer is and what their brand stands for. Is their pricing inexpensive or expensive? Is the availability common (McDonald's) or exclusive (Ritz-Carlton)? Don't automatically think a Ritz Carlton brand is more profitable than a Motel 6 brand. The lowest price points can absolutely be the most profitable. The heart of branding is how to segment customers and what to market or feed them. For example, Motel 6's trademark line, "We will leave the light on for you," is cute but lets you know not to expect much more. Great is like a prelude to a kiss or promise to customers. Another bone here – the longest filibuster in American history was by Senator Strom Thurmond of South Caroline; it lasted twenty-four hours and eighteen minutes and he brought with him to the podium cough drops and malted milk tablets. It was a bore.

Except for the very best companies like GoDaddy, business branding can be boring, but as a Liberal Arts major, I think you can see the best branding has been in music. Cher's real name was Cherilyn Sarkisian, and she cut it and just made it Cher, which became a brand of freedom. It said to her followers, "it's all about me." Listen to Half Breed and you see how the song was foundational to her brand Cher. Madonna's brand took it to another generational level. When someone owns a brand space, you can't copy it – one of the biggest mistakes in business. You have to recast it for an underserved customer segment.

Clown Car –

A group whose size is ridiculously excessive in number especially for the stated purpose and function of the group and whose effectiveness is comically questioned. The planning committee has added another member to its clown car, so look for more delays.

Dashboard –

An electronic overview of the reports and metrics you care about most in the business unit.

Downside –

The potential loss or fallout from risks taken.

Edutainment –

Providing entertainment to an audience so that they don't care if they're being pitched to buy something.

Gamify –

Adding a game feature to a website or product experience that often gives rewards for additional use.

Gartner Group –

The God of advisory groups, providing insights and research, for high pay, to marketing executives and other senior executives. The Gartner Group became the authority on who is best in class in every category of tech.

Ghosted –

Meaning a prospect suddenly stopped responding to any form of contact.

Golden Handcuffs –

A generous compensation agreement to lock in key employees for the long haul with severe penalties if they leave.

Golden Parachute –

Generous exit benefits for employees if the company is sold or merged or hires a replacement for those employees.

Groupthink –

A disparaging word in business circles that describes a lack of individual creativity or responsibility in a group interaction and is often apparent in staff or team meetings.

Guru –

A self-proclaimed expert or somebody in the market who has been recognized as having an in-depth knowledge in a particular experience, topic, or business.

Influencer –

People on Instagram, YouTube, or other social media channels who have amassed a large following and can market to them. Many companies hire influencers now to post a photo or video using their products or services, in the hopes they will see an uptick in sales from the followers of the influencer.

Iterate –

A fancy way of saying that you are tweaking something that isn't right yet.

Launch –

To have a website or a new product go live.

LOC (Letter of Credit) –

A document from a bank that guarantees payment, often used in construction projects or international trade.

Magic Quadrant –

A highly sought after Gartner report listing worth millions if you're listed anywhere on the quad, but the primo space is the upper right-hand corner that proclaims companies as leaders in the categories of Visionary, Execution, Niche, or Challenger. You only get into that magic quadrant when you work your butt off and invest heavily into Gartner.

The company I founded called STI Knowledge made the top right-hand corner and we were the smallest company in that coveted corner. For the first time, we exhaled in a whiff of honor when we realized the company next closest to us in revenue had two billion dollars in sales. We finally made it with the big boys as we were named both a visionary and execution leader.

North American Outsourcing Magic Quadrant

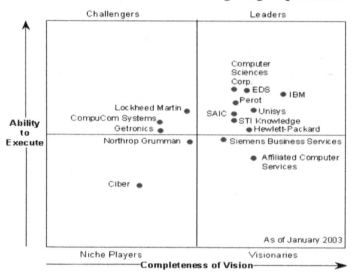

Source: Gartner Research
Images may be subject to Copyright

Milestones —

Performance goals by which employees' success is measured.

NPS: Net Promoter Score —

A metric for assessing customer loyalty for a company's brand, product, or service.

Omnichannel —

A fancy way to describe a multi-prong approach to touching customers, via email, direct mail, television, social media, and so on.

Responsive Design —

A website built for optimal viewing across all devices.

Social Media —

Facebook, Instagram, Pinterest, Twitter, YouTube, Snapchat, LinkedIn, The only two you need to worry about are Twitter and LinkedIn. If you don't have accounts with these services, sign up now.

Snapshot —

Instead of grinding through tons of data, it's just a quick slice of information to represent where things stand.

Strip Line —

Internal sales smack to say you will get a yes or no answer from a prospect.

Sweat Equity —

Means ownership of something in exchange for work done. Used a lot more in marketing than finance as it is usually more of a recruitment tool.

Template —

A file that serves as the skeleton or framework. Your starting point when creating new documents.

Tribe —

A Seth Godin term referring to like-minded team members or customers. Try not to use this expression more than once every six months.

Upside —

The potential profit or pay beyond the investment of resources.

User Experience Design —

Technology designed with a user-friendly experience in mind.

Vlogger —

A video blogger.

CHAPTER 6

NEGOTIATION: HOW TO GET TO YES FOR A WIN-WIN

In business, you are going to be trading and persuading all day long and it is not all about money. It also includes the negotiation of ideas, tasks, and priorities, etc. Successful negotiations require creative marketing, sales, and strategy. You can't just pound the table and having an impressive sounding job title only gets you so far. Good news, bad news routine – bad news is that not many people in business are good negotiators. Good news is, you can be the best negotiator in the room if you follow these eighteen bullet point tactics.

1. *Never let the other side see you sweat.*

2. *Find out the other party's agenda and embrace it.* It is imperative to understand the point of view of the person you will

be negotiating with by asking yourself these questions: What represents a successful result for him/her? What will constitute a win for him/her in a negotiation session? How can you make him/her look better? You don't get to enjoy a victory lap in negotiations until you have walked a mile in the other person's shoes.

3. *Represent the market reality for which you are asking.* Sam Walton drove a Ford F-150 truck because he wanted to look like a low-cost seller. You have to be who you say you are 24/7 and not just during work hours. If you are selling yachts, you better look like a yachtsman. Look like the money you are asking for.

4. *Know if time is working for or against you.* During the late stages of the Vietnam War, the Viet Cong government knew Americans could not stomach watching the tragedies of war on television, so they knew they had to outlast negotiations. While our Secretary of State, Henry Kissinger, wanted to make a deal to end the war, the Viet Cong had long talks and negotiations over where everyone sat.

5. *Never split the difference.* There are many ways to negotiate. "The reasonable person" theory says that a reasonable person should ask for money or conditions that are very close to what he/she actually wants, and that is close to what is fair. The problem is that those two things are often very different.

If the market value for a service is $100,000, and the employee asks for $500,000, and the employer offers $95,000, then splitting the difference makes no sense. In a situation like that, if you simply split the difference, you would end up with a bizarrely unfair result. At that point, the employer has to assume that she is not dealing with a serious negotiator, because there is no validity to the $500,000 request.

6. *Sell your story, not your values.* Whoever has the best story often wins. President Abraham Lincoln, a lawyer before he became a politician, sold the story of a log splitter born in a cabin. It's a good story if you were campaigning for President in 1860. He used his story to negotiate the support of his presidential candidacy; his values were an added bonus. What is your story? Write it down. Create a video. Document it. Think of it as the equivalent of a storybook negotiation that details facts and figures to support your market reality.

7. *Negotiating is not about what is fair.* You cannot allow negotiations to turn on personal circumstance. Negotiations should be based on the market value of what you do or what you are buying. For example, some football players would be happy playing in the NFL for next to nothing. But that is not the market reality. Professional football generates tremendous revenue and players take enormous

risks. That is why the majority are paid millions to play the game.

8. *When you are going to lose, do not go for broke.* Get creative instead. You never push a totally losing argument to the end. When you start to face a deadlock, and you know that you cannot win, it is time to back off. That is when entrepreneurs push themselves to think of a new way to solve the problem. Instead of just speechifying, think of ways to create new value.

9. *Explain the past, but sell the future.* Your company's past is memorialized in numbers, facts, and data comparables. Don't try to resell that reality. Explain it so all parties understand it. For example, "Gross margins declined because we invested in I.T. infrastructure," is an explanation of the past. "We will now be able to scale and franchise 100 stores over the next year," is selling the future of "Entrepreneur Heaven."

10. *Know how to deal with deadlock.* Assume that in any negotiation process, an impasse will occur. Turn on the high emotional I.Q. Disarm the other side and do not blow up like a "Brilliant Jerk" out of "Corporate Hell." (Stay tuned for more info on these in Chapter 8.) Step back for an hour or two. Sometimes it could involve shifting to a new setting and changing the context of the negotiation. I go to see a movie, or I read an entire newspaper, and when I come back, everything is different.

11. *Make the first offer.* The old thought on this is the other side goes first. No, go first and frame the debate and set the parameters of your market reality.

12. *Understand the people, not just their stances.* Know who is on the other side of the table: tendencies, strong points, background.

13. *Disarm the opposition.* Humor and sincerity are the best tonics to dilute animosity and opposition.

14. *When things turn overly personal, head back to "strictly business."* Do not deny that negotiations can get emotional and personal. Also, remind yourself that it is natural for someone to try to save money or get his or her way. Do not let that attitude be a startling revelation when you sit down to negotiate. Make it your job to keep things strictly business.

15. *Sandbagging is inevitable – get ready for it, and don't be afraid to do a little bit of your own.* We do not feel satisfied unless we have gone through a process that involves bargaining back and forth. All human beings like to feel some sense of achievement. They want to feel as if they have won something, and they also like to justify the time they spent in the negotiating process. Fudging is when your first proposal needs to be higher than what you would ultimately take, and sandbagging is when you understate what you can do.

16. *Negotiations are not a search-and-destroy mission.* The one sure thing that I know about business is that, if you have your foot on someone else's neck, at some point in the future, that person will have his foot on your neck. We want a win-win situation. If your side of the winnings is going to be big, do not clean the table and just leave. Take your winnings and give the appearance and action that you want the other side to earn and win her way back. Make it a positive loss and an earned opportunity ahead.

Always see the future. You never want to treat any one negotiation as the last opportunity for a win-win result. You need to look at the whole picture and at the entire relationship (especially at your long-term interests) as opposed to obsessing over the current situation. Even when you win, you cannot afford to lose that perspective.

17. *The art of closing a deal is to stay focused through the very end.* There are critical points at the end when nearing terms that need to be negotiated and documented. That is when you should draw on your mental discipline. "Corporate Hell" concerns itself with what time the last flight leaves, or what it would be like to get home early to play golf with the boss. Do not get trapped. Remain focused until the very end.

18. *Phone vs. Email in Critical Sales/Negotiation Situations.* When you're in the middle of a big project or negotiation and receive email questions from the customer or a colleague,

never, ever respond back with an email. Instead, ALWAYS "pick up the phone" and address their questions. There is often more behind their questions than is obvious. Talking over the phone, you get a lot more interaction time and you're going to structure a better response/deal. This both improves the outcomes and strengthens the relationship.

We are not naïve enough to believe that everyone will negotiate in good faith. Lowball or "submarine offers" are real world negotiation tactics. If someone throws you a lowball offer, look at it first as an interested customer, not as an insult. If you are going to make a lowball offer, send it with a letter of explanation stating why you see your offer as the market reality. (We will talk a lot more about this in Chapter 9.) The note shows you respect the other side. On the other hand, a naked lowball offer is an insult to the other person and process.

Don't count on getting what you deserve in business. You get what you negotiate.

CHAPTER 7

STARE INTO THE LAKE AND KEEP YOUR MOUTH CLOSED

Business communication has three parts. One is talking, one is listening, and the other is knowing when to keep your mouth shut – whoever speaks first loses.

Business is a lot of talking, meetings, and clarifications. One of the most valuable lessons that an employee can learn is that there are three times that you must always keep your mouth closed, and here they are:

1. Never contradict your boss in public.
2. After the sale is made, say thank you and get out of the room.
3. Remain silent after you have given your price.

The hard part is when the other person has learned the same lesson.

I once had to endure the longest pause of my life with a guy who is a highly successful software entrepreneur. As it turned out, he didn't like two things: people and talking. And he has learned to play both dislikes to his advantage. I should have realized this when he had a mutual acquaintance call me to introduce us.

The acquaintance started the conversation this way: "He is eccentric, a little weird, maybe a lot weird, but he is brilliant. He has built a very profitable business where his software serves a platform for small mortgage companies. He is ready to take a solo boat trip across the Atlantic, so he wants to get out. See if you can help him, and here is his number."

I called the number and got one of his colleagues, who seemed a little scattered and odd. She was busy baking a cake at work. This would be what we call a "red flag," in the business world – a warning sign that danger is ahead or at least a rocky road. She said the owner had told her to take care of all of my arrangements. I was a little concerned because I was expecting to talk to him first but, bam, before I knew it, there was money in my account for my flight and fees. It wasn't cheap. I'm in Atlanta, and he's on a lake in Nevada.

A couple of weeks later, I flew out and picked up a rental. As I drove to the lake, I realized that I was headed not toward an office, but a residential home. It was getting dark, and I had trouble finding it. I started feeling uneasy, but I pushed on and finally found the place.

There were no lights on. I knocked and rang the doorbell, but got no response. As I started to walk away, a guy stuck his head out and just looked at me. He didn't have a shirt on. I was caught off guard and kind of pointed in the air to the east and said, "I am from Atlanta." He said, "OK, come in." As we were walking through the dark house, it occurred to me that I had no idea what game he was playing; I just knew that I was losing.

We walked through the house and out on to a deck overlooking the lake. There was no moon so it was pitch black. He looked up in the air and asked, "What have you done?" I started thinking that this was not going in my favor so I gave him the short version of my bio and tried, nervously, to remind him why I was there: "You asked me to come out?"

He looked me straight in the eyes and said, "How much do you want?" I decided right then, in a split second, that I was not going to ask him, "Do you mean to sell your company?" I was sure he wanted me to ask, but I was not going to do it. I knew this was the time to name a number and shut my mouth. I raised my voice just a little and said, "For a company of your revenue size, it will be 250 grand." I said nothing about conditions, commissions, retainers, or anything else.

And the silence began. He looked at me, shook his head, cocked one leg up on a deck rail, and just stared out into the lake. So I cocked my leg up on the deck rail and stared along with him. I knew this – if I said anything, it would be a wasted trip. For almost ten minutes, although it seemed far longer, we both stood there staring into the lake, not saying a word. Finally, the agony ended. He took his foot off the rail and said, "OK, let's do it."

As I was driving back to the airport, I thought of something my grandmother said to me when I told her I was going off to college. "When you get up there," she said, "I want you to do more praying and less talking." I must confess that I did not do much praying in college, but I made up for it as I was walking through that house and standing on the deck staring into the lake, just keeping my mouth shut.

When business babble is always in long supply, silence can be golden.

Another bone – Bill Clinton, then governor of Arkansas and rising star, was allotted fifteen minutes to speak at 1988 Democratic national convention. Instead, he spoke for thirty-three minutes, interrupted by boos and chants to stop and finally cheers when he said "In Conclusion." In contrast, Lincoln's 272 word Gettysburg address lasted three minutes and when Lincoln sat down, he leaned over to the person sitting next to him and said "That speech won't scowl," which is what you saw about a plow that can't till the soil from its blade. Brevity is a virtue in human communications.

CHAPTER 8

DEALING WITH
THE BRILLIANT JERK

In your new workplace, you will highly likely find yourself dealing with a "Brilliant Jerk." This person is typically a specialized, high producing performer and usually, a prick. Brilliant Jerks are not necessarily brilliant businesspeople. It's just that they're brilliant at one thing. Follow my instructions in this chapter and you will never have a Brilliant Jerk ruin your day or worse, your career.

Don't confuse a jerk with a Brilliant Jerk. Two different characters – jerks come and go. Brilliant jerks are sticky ones and seem to stay forever. I have to teach you how to spot the Brilliant Jerk. Recently, I was helping a group of twenty-five doctors thrash out their shared values as they tried to become a real company.

Toward the front of the room, I spotted the Brilliant Jerk. He was the one doctor who dampened the unity with subtle but consistent complaining about why the group couldn't do some things and shouldn't do others. When he spoke, everyone became quiet and listened – not out of excitement for what he was going to say, but out of respect. Yes, the doctors had respect for the Brilliant Jerk.

Here's why: He was always the first to cover for doctors who were on call. He was always the first to volunteer to work on holidays. He had the most articles published by the American Medical Association. He was the first to get new training and share it with others one-on-one. And by the way, he was the highest revenue producer of all the doctors in the group. In fact, he was producing twice the revenue of some of the doctors. He had been the third doctor to join the group and without his revenue, the start-up could not have been successful.

But here's the problem: While he had performed brilliantly for the start-up, he was not performing brilliantly for a company that was trying to grow. The brilliant start-up talent had become the Brilliant Jerk.

Most high-growth companies start with two or three founders and employees who have a common idea and are passionately committed to the mission. The cause creates shared values among the group and work is fun. Most days, everyone feels like part of the team and does great work; some days it feels like "Survivor" – as when you are working nights and weekends to ensure that the start-up is still in business come Monday morning. At this stage, everyone is important. Decisions are usually made when everyone is in the room or at least within earshot.

But then, with this kind of commitment, hard work, and passion, the company starts to grow and maybe even double in size and revenue. All of a sudden, instead of being part of a scout troop, you are riding a rocket. Work is fun and exciting but with constant turbulence, and all of the participants have to give it their all to keep the rocket in orbit and in alignment on the new mission of growth. Inevitably, at least one of the founders or early superstars will not like the new mission. This person will still want to be the Brilliant Talent of the start-up – instead of being a contributor on the rocket, where everyone has to step up to newly defined roles and where new superstars are made. But instead, he now becomes the Brilliant Jerk.

I had a Brilliant Jerk when I was building my company, STI Knowledge, into a brand. When we hired him, we hired over our heads. He had juice. We marveled at his manic performance, which often propelled all of us. When we had a crisis, he could solve it. Yes, he could have taken bigger jobs at bigger salaries, but he chose to work with rebels. He knew we were right in our vision and mission, and he knew we could not do it without him. But in trying to maintain his glory, he struggled to let us go and grow.

The growth phase required the addition of staff members, systems and structure that changed the dynamics of the company. While the Brilliant Jerk was a high-tech genius, the new stars were being made in areas like sales, marketing, and education. He felt left out. He was no longer needed in every meeting. He could not simply pop into the chief executive's office four or five times a day like old times, and the new processes and systems hindered and even prevented him from being the savior. Right before our eyes, the Brilliant Talent became the Brilliant Jerk.

I have listened to Brilliant Jerks proclaim, "I am the one who is always on call, who drives the most revenue, who is here on weekends, and who has the knowledge." And the Brilliant Jerk speaks the truth. But I have also seen him stick his head in the door and deflate an entire management team. A growth company needs enablers, not disablers.

So here's the right answer. If you're the boss, get rid of the Brilliant Jerk as fast as you possibly can. If you're not the boss, stay away from the Brilliant Jerk as much as you possibly can.

If a Brilliant Jerk is an equal or colleague, the best strategy is to be business-like during business hours. You do not need to like them or hang out with them after work. Do not let them bring you down in any way, shape, or form.

CHAPTER 9

CAPITALISM IS NOT PERFECT, BUT IT'S BETTER THAN EVERYTHING ELSE OUT THERE

"The entrepreneur always searches for change,
responds to it, and exploits it as an opportunity."
—Peter Drucker

For all the left-leaning Liberal Arts majors and the like, practice reading the quote above, even if the first few times you have to hold your nose. Here is the good news – exploitation is often a good thing. Entrepreneurs like Herb Keller, founder of Southwest, exploited the aviation industry love of itself rather than the customer who was paying to fly. Starbucks exploited the fact that coffee shops were more interested in customer rotation (known as "turning tables") than customer hospitality. Starbucks found an opportunity to step in where they saw that hole. Here is a good thing for you to figure out – what is your company exploiting? Nine times out of ten, it will be another company's failure to serve a customer or a new market to serve altogether. If it's exploitation to harm, look for another job.

Capitalism is not perfect, but it has lifted more people out of poverty and upstream into society than any other economic system in the history of mankind. In half a generation, families go from being impoverished immigrants to the top of society, based on hard work, merit, and honestly a little luck. Don't be seduced by socialism – it's a classic case of the "grass always looks greener on the other side." Take five minutes and Google the following: Soviet Union, Communist China, Cuba, and now Venezuela. I'll wait.

The biggest offenders of Capitalism is actually not Socialists but the crowd that brought us too big to fail and the pay for play democracy that exists in Washington D.C. today. However, that is having broken people in important positions, not a broken system. It is also quite easy to make the case, the biggest defender of Capitalism has been the likes of Franklin D. Roosevelt who saw the system needed a safety net, rules and fair playing field which means giving a nudge here and there to people of lesser means.

Here's another bone – in a capitalistic system, people pay for convenience, like drive-thrus and room service. Unfortunately, one convenience is costing us – plastic. Plastic was discovered in 1907 by Leo Hendrix in search of materials to replace ivory in billiard balls. Over eight billion tons of plastic have been produced since WWII. Plastic persists in the environment for thousands of years and has brought considerable damage to our oceans and shame to humans. An entrepreneur could exploit our rightful shame by developing a replacement, recycle-able, and biodegradable product.

The standard of Communism is for employees of the state to look down and frown at their feet. The shared value of Capitalism is confidence; head up with a smile – all the more important in a capitalistic career than knowing the difference between simple interest and compound interest. Emily Post said it best: "To make a pleasant and friendly impression is not only good manners, but equally good business."

Many point to the financial crisis of 2008 as the big example of how capitalism failed. Quite the contrary, in the 2008 financial crisis, banks got greedy and loaned money to people who could not pay them back. Capitalism actually worked beautifully. It was going to put the bad banks out of business, which would wipe away all of their built-in advantages and cultivated new innovative banks to replace them.

Even in a capitalistic system, it is not all based on merit. Companies are still very much like communities and societies. You have got to understand a big part of the capitalistic corporate culture is: who gets the credit and who looks good. The boss wants the credit, no matter what they tell you. And what would happen if your boss's boss took credit directly from you? What should you do about it? Take this example from Griffin, who started as an intern with me and landed on Wall Street right after graduation.

A company-wide email was sent out expressing an issue with a spreadsheet that would take a long number of hours and involve many people to correct the issue. Griffin sees the spreadsheet and fixes the problem nearly immediately and responds back to his boss's boss, the one who sent the initial email addressing the problem, that the problem is now fixed. The bosses boss then sends a follow up email to the entire company saying that the problem has been resolved but fails to give any credit to Griffin. (What would you do?) Well, Griffin got up and went directly into the boss's boss's office with a calm attitude and a smile and inquired why he did not receive credit for fixing the problem. The big boss told him he would get that kind of credit after he had been around for a year or more -not what I would have said to a new employee but fair enough – honesty on both sides without any drama. It would have been wrong for Griffin to let it slide without a whimper just like it would have been wrong for him to raise the issue in an email or a group meeting. Griffin has skills – notice he did not go in like a victim but like a winner with a smile on his face and a good disposition. If he had said nothing, no confidence would have been the look. When the boss told him plainly he was basically cheated out of the credit because he was too green (new) for recognition, Griffin said OK and dropped it rather than whine. At work, don't look at every slight of injustice as the next Brown v. Board of Education, a significant landmark decision that changed the country. Let it go.

Takeaways:
- Don't contradict your boss in public.
- Don't ask him why you didn't get credit in public.
- Personally addressing the bosses boss in a professional and polite manner will earn you respect as well as put a face to a name.
- It would have been wrong for Griffin not to have said anything and let it slide. At that time, he would not have earned any respect or gotten facial recognition.

Set aside who gets the credit, capitalism works like a charm if the company is focused on the customer. Here's the best customer service lesson you will ever learn. Customers only want three things from any business:
1. Timeliness (No waiting in line.)
2. Defect-free product (Hotel room light bulbs work just as important as view.)
3. Know that you care. (Aspirin at the front desk.)

If they think you truly care, they will give you a break when you come up short on the first two. If they think you don't care, they will become banshees, sheering your brand.

Below the new owners of Advantage | Forbes Books, conducted an independent customer service assessment immediately after they bought my company, Oxford Center for Entrepreneurs.

From: Chief Customer Officer

Date: August 17, 2018 at 10:16 AM EDT

To: Cliff Oxford

Subject: NPS Observations/Trends for Morning Report

Cliff,

Congratulations again on a record-setting NPS score! Since beginning our NPS program here at Advantage in Nov. 2016, we have never seen a score as high as 83 for any business unit.

A score of 83 narrowly beats out Costco's maintained score of 82. Other notable companies you eclipse are Southwest Airlines (62), Amazon (64), Disney (65), Apple (72), and Chik-Fil-A (72).

Thanks,
Ben

What is the secret to building a great brand? Ridiculous responsiveness is a great start. Then a customer service strategy built around three counterintuitive facts: One, focus groups are a waste of time. It is not the customer's job to take time off and tell you what to do.

Two, don't send customers long surveys asking how you did on every transaction or interaction. Spend all that time to exceed their expectations at every touchpoint for what they paid you to do.

Three, finally, customers give you referrals not to help you but first to help themselves or make themselves look good. Don't ask for them. Referrals will come in droves if you show great outcomes.

Just like customers are a reality in a capitalistic society, lowball offers are too as we've already mentioned. Remember, don't get mad, look at it as an interested customer rather than an insult. Here is a way to make a legitimate lowball offer of your own:

Dear Seller:

I'm writing to let you know that I would like to make a bid on your property. I love the area and am committed to buying a house nearby. And your home fits my needs.

But given that my offer is well below your asking price, I also feel I owe you an explanation.

First, consider the big picture. Nationwide, home prices in the first quarter of 2008 fell 14.1 percent compared with the same period a year earlier, according to the S&P/ Case-Shiller U.S. National Home Price Index.

That's the biggest decline in the twenty-year history of the data. And just in case you're wondering, during the housing downturn of the early 1990s, the decline was never worse than 2.8 percent.

Not only that, earlier this month, the National Association of Realtors pointed to the huge number of existing homes on the market. As of the end of April, the total number was 4.55 million. At the rate people are buying right now, that represents an 11.2-month supply.

So buyers have options right now—a lot of them. I'm no different. Your home is great, but it isn't unique. Few homes are. I know this may be hard to hear since you've spent years creating memories here. But you may be waiting a long time if you hope to find a buyer with the same emotional connection that you have.

My mindset is hardly unique. We've all been reading the headlines. The accompanying articles appear prominently in major newspapers and sit on the Web pages where people check their email every day. Everyone sees them, and the psychological impact is real.

Has your real estate agent laid any of this out for you? Maybe so, and you didn't want to believe it. But it's also possible that your agent, afraid of offending you and losing the listing, simply doesn't want to initiate that sort of discussion. It may be worth sitting down for a candid reassessment.

It will be tempting to view my low bid as an insult. Please don't make that mistake. Your home is genuinely appealing, and I wouldn't have written this note unless I was serious about buying it. Getting a firm offer in this market is an accomplishment. So congratulations!

Oh, and one more thing. You presumably need someplace to move. My guess is that you'll find these same points compelling when it's your turn to buy. You just might succeed in buying for a better price, too.

I look forward to hearing from you soon.

Yours truly,
The Realist

Likewise, if you are on the receiving end of a low ball offer, don't pick up the phone and scream at the potential buyer. Respond professionally. Remember—never let the other side see you sweat.

Dear Bidder:

Thanks so much for your note. I'm truly glad that you like our home as much as we do. You're right that my family and I have many great memories of this place, and we hope someday you will, too.

And I just want you to know that I'm not insulted in any way by your offer. The fact is, none of us are very good at buying and selling homes. We don't do it often, and as much as we know we're not supposed to let emotions get in the way, it's hard not to. After all, few people buy or sell anything else as expensive as a home in their lifetimes.

That said, your offer disappoints me. You seem to believe that I'm not aware of how bad things are out there or that I'm in denial. But I do read the headlines, and I priced the house accordingly. I knew I might have to wait awhile to sell it. I should point out that your data draws on what has already happened in the housing market. Instead, I'd ask you to consider what is about to happen.

One big reason for the falling prices is that it's harder to get mortgages. Lenders went from giving money to anyone with a pulse to demanding higher credit scores and larger down payments. All sorts of buyers simply couldn't make the numbers work anymore. That may now change. Starting June 1, Fannie Mae and Freddie Mac, which buys mortgages from lenders and helps make it possible for them to lend more money, are loosening restrictions on the sorts of loans they'll

buy in many markets. That is supposed to make it easier for people to buy a home with a down payment of 5 percent, or even less. Many more qualified buyers should mean more bids, and I'm willing to wait to see if it turns out that way.

I know you talked about having choices, but presumably, we wouldn't be engaging in this correspondence unless you liked my home best. Given that, I'd ask you to think about something: How often do you find a place that you can actually imagine living in? Sure, there are a lot of other properties out there. But an increasing number are in foreclosure and probably have problems lurking within the walls. So don't let the fear of a falling market keep you out of a home that you truly want.

It's probably obvious by now that I'm not going to counter with a particular number. This doesn't mean that I do not want to negotiate. I'd just like you to consider what I've said and see if you find it convincing. In the meantime, other shoppers who are interested in my home now have a price to beat. So thanks for helping me out with that.

Just one more thing... please take another look at the mortgage calculator you're using and see how your monthly payment will change if you brought your price up a bit. It almost certainly is not going to be enough to break you. But it may be enough to get us to a deal.

I look forward to your reply.

Yours,

The Undaunted

CHAPTER 10

BUSINESS BROTHERS

A s both an academic and practicing entrepreneur, I have studied hundreds of different business models and case studies to explain how start-ups are built into corporations. In short, I want to wisely give you a set of blueprints on how organizationally a company comes together. This will help you know what is going on with your new place of work instead of just seeing a bunch of different departments. I will give you the best business blueprint to understand your company. See the McKinsey 7S Framework chart next page.

For bodies, cars, jet planes, or just about anything to work properly, all parts and pieces have to be in alignment and so do companies. Here is a crash course in business anatomy and how people gel together to produce a product to change lives and a profit to make shareholders happy.

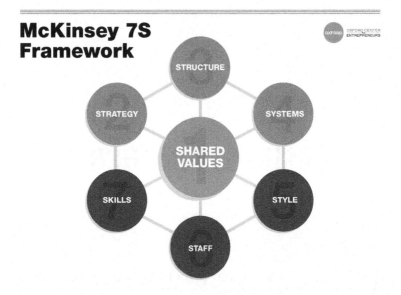

McKinsey 7S Framework

STRUCTURE

STRATEGY

SYSTEMS

SHARED VALUES

SKILLS

STYLE

STAFF

OXFORD OXFORD CENTER ENTREPRENEURS

© 2015 Oxford Center for Entrepreneurs. All Rights Reserved.

A successful business is built around the alignment of the 7 S's above working and weaving together. The big point is no S is more important than the other and all are in alignment are none are – six out seven don't cut it any better than three out of four aligned wheels on a car does. For example, in the early days, Southwest's shared values centered around "wheels up" so families could spend more time on vacation instead of riding Greyhound (more important than captains and uniforms); their strategy was low fares and systems was seat yourself – it too expensive to have a frequent flyer program and seating systems. You can feel the alignment like you can feel the love in Lion King. The style was fun. Structure informal and staff's mindset – catch somebody doing something right was their motto. Skills sought after for the company was gate agents – at the time considered a bottom floor position at other airlines. After you complete a three-month quarter at your company – here is a homework assignment – align the 7S below.

1. **Shared Values/Superordinate Goals**
   a. Guiding concepts, fundamental ideas around which a business is built must be simple, usually stated at an abstract level, and have great meaning inside the organization even though outsiders may not see or understand them.

2. **Strategy**
   a. Actions a company plans in response to or anticipation of changes in its external environment.

3. **Structure**
   a. Basis for specialization and coordination influenced primarily by strategy and by organization size and diversity.

4. **Systems**
   a. Formal and informal procedures that support the strategy and structure (systems are more powerful than they are given credit).

5. **Style/Culture**
   a. The culture of the organization, consisting of two components:

    i. Organizational Culture: the dominant values, beliefs, and norms, which develop over time and become relatively enduring features of organizational life.

   ii. Management Style: more a matter of what managers do than what they say. How do a company's managers spend their time? On what are they focusing attention?

6. **Staff**

   a. The people/human resource management. Processes used to develop managers, socialization processes, ways of shaping basic values of management cadre, ways of introducing young recruits to the company, ways of helping to manage the careers of employees.

7. **Skills**

   a. The distinctive competences – what the company does best, ways of expanding, or shifting competencies.

Even when 7 S's are aligned, companies don't go up forever. Like a rollercoaster, companies go up and down, and the good ones figure out how to go back up among cutthroat competition, changing markets, and endless investments to grow.

The charts below show how a company will start as a venture firm and then mature through three different growth stages: hypergrowth, human scale, and financial scale. Like a rollercoaster that runs off the rails, companies do the same when they go into "no man's land," known when growing revenues increase the rate of expenses faster than profits and should be considered as dire as a rip tide warning on the beach. However, don't bail on a company that is rising like a rocket and then takes a dip if you see management making adjustments to adapt to challenges. Many employees do, and they miss the opportunities of the next race to the top. Look at charts below and find your company as soon as you can.

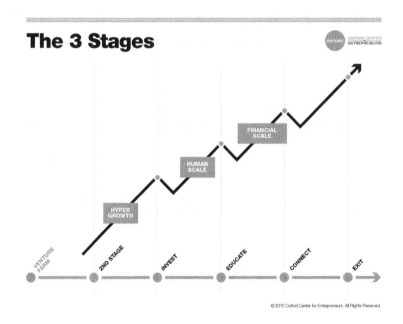

The 3 Stages Hyper Growth

OXFORD · OXFORD CENTER for ENTREPRENEURS

No matter if your company is like a consumer power house Home Depot or a Silicon Valley high-tech riser, all successful companies go through respectively 3 growth stages: Hyper Growth, Human Scale and Financial Scale. As the graph indicates, a successful startup leaves the Venture Farm into the Hyper Growth Stage when a company figures out how to deliver a unique solution to an underserved market. The rapid momentum of additional customers and increased revenue propels the company to a fast-rise most often above its own limitations. In short, revenue overcomes all problems for a time period. Shared Values and Style are top priorities in the Hyper Growth stage. READ MORE.

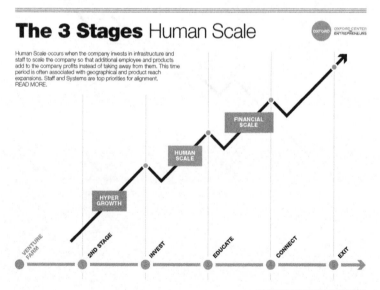

FINANCIAL SCALE

HUMAN SCALE

HYPER GROWTH

VENTURE FARM · 2ND STAGE · INVEST · EDUCATE · CONNECT · EXIT

The 3 Stages Human Scale

OXFORD · OXFORD CENTER for ENTREPRENEURS

Human Scale occurs when the company invests in infrastructure and staff to scale the company so that additional employee and products add to the company profits instead of taking away from them. This time period is often associated with geographical and product reach expansions. Staff and Systems are top priorities for alignment. READ MORE.

FINANCIAL SCALE

HUMAN SCALE

HYPER GROWTH

VENTURE FARM · 2ND STAGE · INVEST · EDUCATE · CONNECT · EXIT

The 3 Stages Financial Scale

OXFORD CENTER ENTREPRENEURS

Financial scale is the time period of growth where the company makes investments and systems to replicate and automate data decisions that add to profits of the company faster than the rate of cost. The company exploits its competitive advantage to become a market leader. Structure and Strategy are top priorities during this period. READ MORE.

The 3 Stages Beyond Chaos

OXFORD CENTER ENTREPRENEURS

How do high flyers become flame out failures?

If a company of high performers leaves during Hyper Growth, chaos overwhelms the company and suppresses the wide-open market opportunity. Sudden market change alone rarely pushes a company off course of Hyper Growth. High performers adapt.

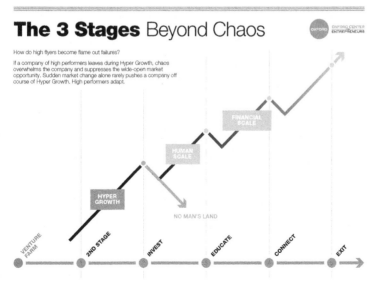

CHAPTER 11

HOW TO DEAL
WITH A BAD BOSS

I've got news for you. You have at least an 80% chance of having a horrible boss – just don't quit over it. Don't let a bad boss stop you. By the way, the bigger the company, the higher the odds of a bad boss, because they hide out in a bureaucracy.

You will leave many meetings with the feeling that you could do the job better than the person who is asking you the questions. Worse news, you will be facing an unconscious, incompetent boss who doesn't know how bad they are. Your meeting will usually end with no decision at all – get used to it and deal with it. Here are the three ways you can identify a bad boss.

1. The boss's desk is a mess, and she can't find the report that you handed to them a few minutes before.

a. Your Response: Sit quietly. Breathe deeply. As you bring your adrenaline under control, you bring a calming tone to you and your new boss.

2. The boss experiences constant interruptions from the telephone or people walking into the office.

a. Your Response: Use those interruptions as opportunities to review what has happened so far and what points you want to make. Also use this time to review the list of questions you want to ask. This is especially important when the boss does not give you the openings you need to sell yourself. Always have a few easy questions prepared to save the situation. Here are some examples:

i. Let the boss choose the location of the next group dinner

ii. Asking their opinion on an already established outcome

3. Two types of questions for bad bosses:

a. Softball question – This is a question with an easy answer that typically glorifies you or your business. If someone throws you a softball question, they are on your side. "Tell me more about why your staff is so great?" They've already acknowledged your staff and they are just giving you a chance to sing some praises.

b. Beach Ball question – This is a question that has an answer already loaded; it should be a "no brainer" for the person answering. For example, if during a sales presentation the CFO says, "Isn't your product the best price on the market?"

Don't let a bad boss be an excuse to do nothing. Let's say you're hired in HR, and everybody is doing everything the same old way. No, you don't want to invent new ways of doing business in what we call "reinventing the wheel," which requires asking for too much permission. The best work in business is repackaged and repurposed old ideas. Take job postings for example.

Most HR teams will post on a job site that they are "hiring for a Senior Account Executive role and are looking for somebody with experience." They will request the applicant send in a resume and cover letter. This would be an opportunity for you to break free from using the same old job type posting and changing it up a bit.

Here is a value-added redo:

CAREERS

[NOW HIRING] Sales Agent, Atlanta, GA

Cliff Co. is a platform that represents authors, scientists, and public intellectuals for keynotes, lectures, and travel. Our exclusive speakers include entrepreneurs and other remarkable individuals who are "making the world a smarter place."

We have grown every year since our inception, ten years ago, and are now hiring an account executive. We're looking for someone to fit into our fast-paced Atlanta office—someone with a strong curiosity and a keen interest in what's hot, what's happening, and what's relevant to audiences. The ideal candidates are voracious readers and pop culture fanatics. But, also—and we can't stress this enough—they are people with amazing sales skills. Candidates must be familiar with, and excel at, the sales process. You must be able to understand and sell intangibles and be tenacious, persistent, and persuasive, on the phone and by email. You must be able to get attention and to hold it, in a helpful and authentic manner.

The job is hard, but it's also fun and meaningful work. You need to be able to prospect, to maintain and grow a client base, to guide a sale from beginning to end, to manage expectations, to meet quotas, to engage fully with buyers, and to speak—with clarity, purpose, and verve—about our roster of world-changing speakers.

If this sounds like a great career opportunity to you, please take a few moments to check out our website.

Then, send us a boring resume as well as an original and fascinating cover letter that highlights your fiercely competitive streak, your many successes, and your quick wit and imagination—a letter, written just for us, which states why you think you'd make the perfect fit at Cliff Co., and vice versa. Please also tell us about one cultural figure who you think is underrated, the last book you read, and a situation from your past that demonstrates your sales ability.

Remember: "add value" without having to reinvent the wheel or ask for permission.

CHAPTER 12

DAY 1 READY AND AFTER

The most important thing I can tell you to do on Day 1 is the same thing I would tell you to do on the last day – if you say you are going to do something, do it. No excuses, even legitimate ones. This will set you apart quickly because the biggest failures in businesses every day are people simply not doing what they promised and this goes for big and small commitments. Both are equally important. Make sure you distinguish between goals and commitments – saying, "I will be at work every day before 8 a.m." is different than saying, "My goal is to double sales."

I am going to hand you a playbook of terms, advice, helpful tips, and even some business etiquette. Keep these in mind as you trek through your first year in business, and reread them every couple of years. These should not be forgotten.

Don't be a crowd pleaser, kissing babies on the first day. Be ready, but also let the game come to you the first week and when it does, hit that ball out of the park.

You are going to be in meetings with titles a lot bigger than yours, but you're going to have bigger ideas – let the group hear them. After the meeting, come up with a checklist to get things done, do them, and you are in business.

If you have a family event like a wedding you need to attend, get this understanding from HR right after you are offered the job. Do not ask for extra days off in your first calendar year. Yes, you should forgo your usual boys' or girls' trip. Make your job a higher priority over taking off early on a Friday to go out drinking with friends. This is business.

Don't wait to be told what to do – look around and beware of your surroundings. Figure out what needs to get done and jump in or volunteer to help. If you can only work as directed, your career will be in the range of the NFL – not for long.

Don't bring tuna fish to cook in the microwave and stink up the whole place. It will take six months before people forget that you burned a bag of popcorn in the break room. And don't eat a sloppy joe at your desk even if others are. Bring or buy a smoothie. But not the extra large Slurpee size. No larger than medium size cup at your desk.

Be nice to the I.T. people and load up on favors to them. If your systems are not working, neither are you.

Get a good night's sleep starting three days before your first day. You are going to be nervous the night before so the two previous nights are just as critical. Advil PM is a good solution the night before if you have at least seven hours before getting up.

Stay out of small talk, period. This is especially true when you are first coming in the door. Say hello, smile, and get to work.

The first rule of attending networking events is – don't complain about how much you don't like networking events.

Don't be bashful. Say hello to everyone, but not like you are running a Boston mayoral campaign. Understated elegance goes a long way in business in the long term.

Show from day one you can GSD – Get S*#& Done.

If your boss or big boss asks for a volunteer to take notes, raise your hand.

If you want to succeed in business, you are going to have to kiss some ass. Just know how – it is not just telling everyone they are great. Do it with reciprocity and ridiculous responsiveness.

Telling the head of AP they are wonderful will get a weird look, a half-hearted smile, and a slighted thank you. However, if you say something like, "I was in accounting today and Paul said you were great," you will get a big smile, a thanks, and an "I have always liked Paul." Reciprocity is the most basic emotion in a relationship and it is why you don't want to burn bridges and use all your lifeboats. You will go down.

When it comes to sucking up, your ears in business are better than any other part. Listen to what people have to say and make them successful without them asking.

Sell people on what they are already sold. Just package it for them. Business is not a non-profit cause.

No whining. Period. Even if someone screams at you for something you didn't do, suck it up and move on.

Don't be shocked to discover in large corporations, the higher you go, the duller and dumber people are.

It's front line people who get stuff done. For example, at UPS we had great clerks, drivers, and culture.

When I asked a CEO how he made it to the top, he told me that he was always in the room for the big/pivotal decisions being made, but the decision never rested on his input alone. That way when the decisions made had a positive outcome, he was always involved. If it turned out to be a bad decision, it was not his alone.

Don't think anybody at your job is going to think you are great just because you can find problems. Problems are everywhere in every business. Instead, your mindset should be on outcomes, solutions, resolutions, and how to conclude.

If you start something, finish it. If you say you are going to do it, do it. No excuses.

Don't use profanity. You don't have to be a stick in the mud, so you can say, "F that," once in a while...with a smile...and in the right setting. Never use the actual word. Don't be the one that is always saying "GD this" and "GD that."

Show up early. Leave late. At my first company, we created a new acronym FILO – First In Last Out.

Act like an owner, which includes turning off the lights if you are the last to leave.

Eliminate recurring problems.

Look ahead and leave yourself an out.

You are either adding profits to the company or taking from them.

Other than holidays and PTO (paid time off), do not ask for any extra days unless it's a family or medical emergency.

If you get a parking ticket on company business, don't expense it. Pay it.

Don't chase dollars on expense accounts. Keep it clean and give the benefit of the doubt to the company.

Make money for the company.

Smile with sincerity and express empathy but don't let your liberal learnings go too far. Don't get uptight over somebody's feelings getting hurt or somebody was offended by a decision.

Invest time with your tailor, your nutritionist, and your gym.

Being "attractive" in business is not just about looks. It's being well put together, – clothing, smile, attitude, and even appearance. Well put together people get paid more and promoted more. Sorry to break it to you.

Walk with a brisk pace.

If your boss gives you an assignment, turn it around with urgency.

Don't be the early bird for every meeting, but be prompt for every meeting.

Let your boss be involved in easy lay-up decisions, like what city to hold the conference.

Only bring one problem at a time when meeting with your boss.

Be kind and always be on the sunny side.

Position yourself as a proponent of win-win or no deal.

Be ridiculously responsive.

Sleep at least seven hours per night and invest in a great mattress. Science shows sleep is a potent pharmacy for the body and sleep promotes brain creativity.

Exercise at least 150 minutes per week.

Put recyclable straws in the break room.

Sustainability is sexy, so no sermons.

A silent Riviera is an excellent form of meditation.

Let the crimes of capitalism go. Don't tell anybody that you're a socialist.

I still say leave politics and religion at the door.

Don't end or start a conversation with "I don't understand."

Remember to have fun and visit family.

Never say "I'm tired," "I'm afraid," "I'm timid," or "I couldn't care less." Don't be a downer, have a negative undertone, be pissed off, or have suppressed anger.

What goes around comes around.

Start now.

Make others successful.

Take action.

Be curious.

Get to the point.

Embrace negotiations.

Stay out of drama.

Travel to interesting places.

Customers are not always right, but they always come first.

Ideas before results, but then always results.

Trust starts with honesty.

Teamwork is never letting the team down and then picking up the slack when the team needs you.

Put this quote in your back pocket – "The best time to plant an oak tree is yesterday."

I am going to bring you home on this one: Ask not what your company can do for you. Ask what you can do for your company.

CHAPTER 13

YOUR MAIN JOB IS YOUR JOB

Before you can thrive, your #1 job is to survive. Just as countries and companies have to survive, employees have to survive. Take this article I wrote into consideration. It's about companies and employees acting in survival mode and in this case, having to say "F the brand." You will have days like this and just know storms never last. They blow over if you survive.

"F the Brand"

You want a crisis – it's in Jackson, Mississippi, where a company is on the brink of having its credit line frozen and throwing 950 employees on the street. So what do you do? Two things: Get face to face with the decision maker and buy time – don't call. I drove to Jackson to get everybody in the same room.

The bank was ready with numbers to show their case – spreadsheets galore. We know how this movie turns out – numbers are not usually on our side at this point, so I spoke up and asked could we get the skunk out of the room – we needed two weeks to find a solution. The bank pointed out the company already had two years to find a solution. My response was, "You got our full attention now, so give us a chance to find a solution we all want." The banker said they would decide later – it was better than a no. Let's go.

The numbers are a mess: Expenses too high, receivables too high, inventory too high and nothing in focus. To find a positive, I bragged about payables – hardly anything over forty-five days. Bank's biggest worry was inventory spoils – items that never sold. The company had over $2 million sitting in a warehouse. I pulled the CEO aside and said, what the hell? Can you unload at a discount? He replied it would hurt the brand. I said F the brand – you are trying to survive here. It took them one call to unload to a discount store for thirty cents on the dollar and we pledged every dollar to the bank.

The bank never gave a hard answer on the freeze but did give us the week, which at least covered that Thursday's payroll. Live another day. Of course, I was worried, but it's different when it's your ass on the line. I got with the CEO and came up with a back-up plan, which by the way included holding the check from the inventory fire sale until we got clarity on credit line or we needed it to make payroll – like swapping hostages.

The next day the CEO called and asked me exactly what I did. Surprisingly the bank offered to refinance their credit line and lower the payment to make it work. I told the CEO to take it because I had not done a thing. Two days later, the bank was in the headlines: "Sold." Lucky. Wild guess is they decided to punt and let the next owner deal with it. I felt like dancing on a pony keg.

OK, go survive and thrive in business. It can be a blast.

Dedication – In Memoriam of Rebecca Watson

I dedicate this book to two people who had a big impact on my life. I had not always stepped up to their standards, but I tried to get better every day and am deeply grateful for their lessons of love and life.

Memoriam Dedication to **MYRA GARRETT OXFORD**. I was five months old, my sister five years old, and brother six years old when on a hot day my dad brought us all to live with my grandmother at Rt 3 Swamp Rd in Waycross, Georgia. My grandmother was the oldest daughter of seventeen siblings raised on a wild prairie in Woodbury Georgia and had raised seven children of her own, my dad being the youngest. He gave her a $20 bill to buy groceries and had to catch a train to work in High Springs, Florida. We had lost a mother but took our grandmother as a gift from God. Even though she lived the ups and downs of life as a daughter from a prominent entrepreneur on a 1,000 acre farm then a wife of a talented entrepreneur who fell to hard due to drinking during the Great Depression, she rose early every morning with a spring in her step, a smile on her face, and a spirit of love in her heart. She taught us mainly three things: Forgive, forget, and love one another because it all comes back in every whatever way you choose. My brother, sister, and I asked her one day after we got older – had she felt a huge burden when three little ones showed up at her door. She said, "I'm glad you came – I needed the company."

I'd also like to dedicate the book to **REBECCA WATKINS**, who was the spiritual leader of the Oxford Center. Out of nowhere but with worldwide accomplishments, Rebecca showed up at Oxford and was a leader as soon as she walked in the door. She was a manager, a mentor, and a mother to all of us. Rebecca told me my strengths but sensed my shortcomings and walked with me to pick up the pieces whenever I did wrong. She became the go-to person at Oxford for people to make complaints. Members often would tell me, Rebecca loves you and sees no wrong, which was good because what the members were saying about me was mostly true. I needed what all entrepreneurs need, although it is never discussed: enablers of love. Rebecca was my enabler of love, which is why it is so hard for me to think of her now as a memory. So, I don't think. I just know we are in Rebecca's heart, and Rebecca will always be in our hearts.

Made in the USA
Columbia, SC
13 June 2019